TRAPS

CARYL CHURCHILL

Caryl Churchill has written for the stage, television and radio. Her stage plays include *Owners* (Royal Court Theatre Upstairs, 1972); *Objections to Sex and Violence* (Royal Court, 1975); *Light Shining in Buckinghamshire* (Joint Stock on tour, incl. Theatre Upstairs, 1976); *Vinegar Tom* (Monstrous Regiment on tour, incl. Half Moon and ICA, 1976); *Traps* (Theatre Upstairs, 1977); *Cloud Nine* (Joint Stock on tour, incl. Royal Court, London, 1979, then Theatre de Lys, New York, 1981); *Three More Sleepless Nights* (Soho Poly and Theatre Upstairs, 1980); *Top Girls* (Royal Court, London, then Public Theatre, New York, 1982); *Fen* (Joint Stock on tour, incl. Almeida and Royal Court, London, then Public Theatre, New York, 1983); *Softcops* (RSC at the Pit, 1984); *A Mouthful of Birds*, with David Lan, (Joint Stock on tour, incl. Royal Court, 1986); and *Serious Money* (Royal Court and Wyndham's, London, then Public Theatre, New York, 1987).

Caryl Churchill was born in London but spent seven years of her early life in Canada. She now lives in London with her husband. They have three children.

CARYL CHURCHILL

TRAPS

N
H
B

NICK HERN BOOKS

A division of Walker Books Limited

A Nick Hern Book

This edition of *Traps* first published in 1989 by Nick Hern Books, a division of Walker Books Limited, 87 Vauxhall Walk, London SE11 5HJ.

Traps first published in Great Britain in 1978 by Pluto Press Ltd. Published in Methuen's World Dramatists anthology edition 1985.

Set in Baskerville by Book Ens, Saffron Walden, Essex.
Printed by Billings of Worcester
British Cataloguing in Publication Data
    Traps
    I. Title
    822'.914
ISBN 1-85459-095-2

Caryl Churchill

A Chronology of Performed Plays

PLAY	WRITTEN	PERFORMED (s=stage, r=radio, t=television)
Downstairs	1958	1958s
You've No Need to be Frightened	1959?	1961r
Having a Wonderful Time	1959	1960s
Easy Death	1960	1961s
The Ants	1961	1962r
Lovesick	1965	1966r
Identical Twins	?	1968r
Abortive	1968?	1971r
Not . . . not . . . not . . . not . . . not enough oxygen	?	1971r
Schreber's Nervous Illness	?	1972r
Henry's Past	1971	1972r
The Judge's Wife	1971?	1972t
Owners	1972	1972s
Moving Clocks Go Slow	1973	1975s
Turkish Delight	1973	1974t
Perfect Happiness	1973	1973r
Objections to Sex and Violence	1974	1975s
Traps	1976	1977s
Vinegar Tom	1976	1976s
Light Shining in Buckinghamshire	1976	1976s
Floorshow (contributor to)	1977	1977s
The After Dinner Joke	1977	1978t
The Legion Hall Bombing	1978	1979t
Softcops	1978	1983s
Cloud Nine	1978	1979s

Three More Sleepless Nights	1979	1980*s*
Crimes	1981	1981*t*
Top Girls	1980–2	1982*s*
Fen	1982	1983*s*
A Mouthful of Birds		
(with David Lan)	1986	1986*s*
Serious Money	1987	1987*s*
Icecream	1988–9	1989*s*

Traps

When we were casting *Traps*, we found ourselves repeating the same two things to actors as some kind of introduction to the play. First, that it is like an impossible object, or a painting by Escher, where the objects can exist like that on paper, but would be impossible in life. In the play, the time, the place, the characters' motives and relationships cannot all be reconciled — they can happen on stage, but there is no other reality for them. Second, that the characters can be thought of as living many of their possibilities at once. There is no flashback, no fantasy, everything that happens is as real and solid as everything else within the play.

Performance notes

The card trick. The person who chooses a card puts it back on top of the pack. It stays there when the cards are shuffled. If ten cards are dealt off the top of the pack and those cards then put on top of the pack again, the chosen card will be the tenth card.

Mobius strip. Cut a strip of paper and turn one end over before joining the two ends to form a loop. The loop has only one surface. If you cut along the middle of the strip right round the loop, it makes one larger loop.

The jigsaw. I've only occasionally specified where a character should do the jigsaw. Bits can be added at any convenient time by anyone so that it's nearly finished by the end of the play.

Traps was first produced at the Royal Court Theatre
Upstairs, London, in January 1977. The cast was as follows:

SYL, 30	Catherine Kessler
JACK, 20s	Nigel Terry
ALBERT, 35	Anthony Milner
REG, 30	Tim Piggott-Smith
DEL, 20s	Hugh Fraser
CHRISTIE, 20s	Catherine Neilson

JACK *is* CHRISTIE's younger brother, and REG *is her*
husband.

Directed by John Ashford
Designed by Terry Jacobs

TRAPS

ACT ONE

A room with door, window, table, chairs.
Bluish gloom of early evening, the curtain not drawn and the light not on.
Plenty of clutter: large jigsaw half done on the floor, large pot plant, newspapers in various languages, oil lamp, cards, airgun, cake, pile of clothes washed but not ironed, ironing board and iron, towels, broken bowl, guitar, suitcase, picture, carrycot, clock showing real time.
JACK is sitting in a chair, eyes closed. SYL is walking up and down with a baby on her shoulder, getting it to sleep.
A dog barks downstairs as someone comes into the house and comes upstairs.
SYL is afraid the noise will wake the baby. JACK doesn't react.
ALBERT comes in, snapping on the light, banging the door.

ALBERT. Pissing down. . .

> *ALBERT realises SYL is putting the baby to sleep, goes quiet, puts off the light.*
> *SYL puts the sleeping baby in the carrycot and takes it out.*
> *ALBERT puts on the light. He takes off his wet coat and shoes.*

They're after me, Jack.

> *JACK doesn't react to this or the next things ALBERT says.*

Fletcher says, what do I do in the evenings.
He pretends he wants me to watch blue movies.
You see?
What he's doing is try to find out if I belong to any political party.
I'll tell him I got married. You want to go?
You could.
Pissing down out there.
Jack, people are looking at me in a funny way.

JACK*'s eyes are still shut.*

JACK.   Dog barks at you, too.

ALBERT.   It does, exactly, it smells trouble. I used to pat that dog one time. Animals can sense. . . You busy?

JACK.   No, I'll go in my room.

ALBERT.   No, I'll shut up. I'm getting flu, that's all.

               JACK *opens his eyes.*

JACK.   No, I've gone. Keep talking.

ALBERT.   Like earthquakes. Animals sense.

               JACK *gets up.*
               SYL *comes in.*

SYL.   Going out?

JACK.   Just upstairs. All right?

               JACK *goes out.*
               SYL *and* ALBERT *embrace.*

SYL.   She kept waking up all afternoon. I wanted to kill her.

ALBERT.   I'm getting flu.

SYL.   Cold.

ALBERT.   Flu. Syl, people are looking at me in a funny way. Not just that. There's somebody following me. I could have said before. But I wanted to let it pile up till there's no doubt.

SYL.   Babe's got a snuffle.

ALBERT.   Kiddies do.

SYL.   Gave her some gripe water.

ALBERT.   That right? For a cold?

SYL.   What? You give her something. I know you've brought up a fine family. You stop indoors with her then. She likes gripe water.

ALBERT.   Booze, init? Takes after her daddy.

SYL.	Had a swig of gripe water myself. Quarter to three.
ALBERT.	He keeps just the distance he thinks I won't notice. He reckons he's nondescript. Light brown raincoat, medium height, between thirty and forty years of age, dark hair thinning on top, small face, doesn't wear gloves.
SYL.	Do you keep looking round?
ALBERT.	Not all the time, what do you take me for? One day the raincoat, next day the hair, I build it up.
SYL.	It is always the same man?
ALBERT.	Mole on his cheek.
SYL.	Every time?
ALBERT.	Twice is enough.
SYL.	Why don't you stop and let him go by?
ALBERT.	I don't want them to know I know, do I? Lose the advantage.
SYL.	I put her down to sleep at one o'clock, but I knew she wouldn't go off by her face. So I winded her some more and tried again, but I knew she wasn't going to. It's my own fault. If you think your baby's going to cry it cries. But how can you think it's going to go to sleep when it just isn't? So I tried letting her cry. Like people say it's good for their lungs and . . . Why shouldn't she be unhappy for a bit? Everyone else is, I am, cry on. She's got no right. You can't make it perfect for them so why. . . ? But I never can stick her crying. It gets on my stomach.

She isn't looking at ALBERT. *He furtively gets a chocolate biscuit from a packet in the table drawer and quietly and quickly eats it.*

So I get her up and give her some gripe water. And she likes that. It makes her really good.

She lets me put her down and she's not even asleep, just being good. I felt fine. Up till then I was feeling really fine. Quarter to three she starts up again. So this time we both have some gripe water and she won't stop. I give her a shake, Albert. Not hard but . . . a shake. She screamed so hard I had to put her down, I didn't know what to do. So after a bit I put the pram on the wheels and rocked it because often she goes off if she's on a walk but it was raining so hard and my shoe's got this great hole so I put the pram on the wheels and pushed her back and forward, you know, rocking her. . .

ALBERT.   Do stop going on.

SYL.   Boring to listen to?

ALBERT.   A bit.

SYL.   Boring to do.

ALBERT.   I don't come home and tell you every boring thing I did all day. 'Then I thought I must have a piss so I walked along to the toilet.'

SYL.   I've nothing else but boring things to tell.

ALBERT.   Then try saying nothing.

SYL.   Did you know a little baby is three times the size of a human being?

ALBERT.   Come on, love. Saturday day after tomorrow.

SYL.   I've been looking forward to Saturday since Sunday night.

ALBERT.   Best I can do.

SYL.   Because it's completely impossible for you to give up work and look after her and me go out to work for a bit.

ALBERT.   That's right.

SYL.   And why?

ALBERT.   I'd go mad.

SYL.	And me?
ALBERT.	I'm not saying it's fair. Just a fact.
SYL.	What if I went out? What if I just went out? What if I went?
ALBERT.	If you don't want to take care of it, leave it in a church pew. Put it on the steps of the town hall, get taken into care.
SYL.	And a great cure for a headache's to cut off your head.
ALBERT.	You wouldn't earn as much as I do. There's no work. There's nothing you're trained for. You're lucky I'm still in work so you're getting supported. You've no patience, Syl. She'll grow up in no time. I've seen it with mine. They're at school, they're smoking, they've gone. Enjoy it.
SYL.	Something funny happened at quarter to three. I looked at the clock five times and the hands hadn't moved hardly. Got in a panic.
ALBERT.	When I get my cards, I'll stay home and you can try and get a job, all right? It won't be long. When I talk I can tell from their eyes they're thinking. They're working out what the bastard's after. Ah, got it. Wants us to play darts, does he, bleedin' agitator. It's got so if I go in the canteen and say 'Terrible weather for the time of year', it's 'Oh, don't talk politics, Albert.'
SYL.	I do love her and all that. It's just. . .

A knock at the door.
ALBERT gestures to stop SYL saying 'Come in.'
REG puts his head round the door.

| REG. | Oh. Sorry to bother you. I did knock. I expect you didn't hear. |

REG comes in. He is smartly dressed in a heavy coat and carries a very large box of chocolates.

REG.   The good lady said the top two floors. I'm
            looking for Jack Slade.

ALBERT.   Nobody answering to that name.

REG.   Slade. Jack.

ALBERT.   That's right.

REG.   He doesn't live here?

ALBERT.   I hope very much you're calling me a liar. I've
            been wanting to hit somebody all day.

REG.   Joking apart, the lady downstairs said —

ALBERT.   What makes you think you've got the right
            name?

REG.   He's my brother-in-law. Tall scruffy lad.

ALBERT.   He never said he'd got a brother-in-law. Why
            should I believe that?

REG.   You don't deny knowing him then?

ALBERT.   He didn't leave a forwarding address. Moved
            to the country for a healthier life.

REG.   There hasn't been anyone asking for him?

ALBERT.   What's he done?

REG.   Has there been a woman asking for him?

ALBERT.   That would be his own business, wouldn't it?

            REG *approaches* SYL, *who is doing the jigsaw.*

REG.   I don't mind not seeing Jack. I've no interest
            at all. The one I'm looking for is the other
            one. . . Who's looking for Jack herself. I
            believe. I don't want to bother you with the
            details.

ALBERT.   Ask at the pub. He sends postcards to the
            publican.

REG (*to* SYL). I do apologise for taking your time. But if
            someone else turns up looking for Jack, if you
            tell her Reg was here and I'm in the pub, I'd
            be very grateful. No need to let her get you
            into conversation.

SYL.   Reg.

REG.   Most kind.

ALBERT.   Jack isn't married so how could he have a
            brother-in-law?

REG.   I'm the one that's married.

ALBERT.   If Jack's got a sister.

REG.   If she's here all along, hiding, and doesn't
            want to see me, it would be a help to know. I
            haven't got all day.

ALBERT.   Turn left out the front door.

REG (*to* SYL). Tell her Reg came to take her home.

ALBERT.   King's Head on the corner.

            As REG is about to go, JACK *comes in.*

REG.   There seems to be some misunderstanding.

JACK.   No. Amazing. Yeah. What about that?

ALBERT.   Not everyone in uniform is the gasman and
            there's all sorts of plain clothes. You don't
            answer every enquiry made at the door. People
            asking for you by name could lead anywhere.
            The details are transferred to a computer.

REG (*to* JACK). You gave instructions to have me turned
            away. I know there's no love lost. You must
            have expected me, that's the item of interest.

JACK.   Expected is too much. I haven't the confidence.
            I still can't believe you're not a figment.
            Amazing.

REG.   I just dropped by to give Christie a lift home.

JACK.   Christie's not been here for about a year.

SYL (*to* ALBERT). You're getting to be impossible to live
            with.

REG.   She said something about paying you a visit.
            So I drove up.

JACK.   Oh yeah.

REG.   New Volvo since you saw us.

JACK.   Yeah.

REG.   So where is she?

JACK.   I wonder where she's got to.

REG.   I'll be on my way then.

JACK.   If you like, yeah.

REG.   Frankly, Jack, considering the bizarre way I
            was received I find it impossible to believe
            you're telling the truth.

JACK.   She'll most likely come.

REG.   She phoned you up. I never know when she
            gets in touch with you. It comes out later.

ALBERT (*to* SYL). What do you mean by that?

SYL.   It's just true.

ALBERT.   Is that a threat?

SYL.   I didn't think so.

ALBERT.   Who do you talk to in the daytime?

JACK.   Look, Reg, what I was doing when you came.
            I was. . . You're not going to believe this.

REG.   Yes I am.

JACK.   No you're not. No point telling you.

ALBERT (*to* SYL). Eh? Who turns you against me?

REG.   This is typical of your whole attitude towards
            me and you must know how I resent it over
            the years. Totally unjustified scorn bearing no
            relation to my actual character. You make
            trouble where there could be normal accord.

            *JACK takes off his socks, which are not a pair, and
            starts clipping his toenails.*

SYL.   You wouldn't like to do the ironing, Albert?

ALBERT.   When have I ever done the ironing?

SYL.   You tell me.

ALBERT.   I don't think clothes need ironing.

SYL.   Right, I won't bother.

ALBERT.   Look, I'm getting flu.

SYL.   You've a slight snuffle.

ALBERT.   I keep shivering. It doesn't show.

JACK.   Tell you something though, Reg. Yesterday I spotted a kidnap. I saw this guy sort of shouldered into a car, and as they sped off I was thinking 'Was that a gun?'

REG.   Really?

JACK.   Did you know I've got a photographic memory? I did an identikit.

REG.   Which case would that be?

JACK.   No coverage in the media. To bore the villains. You'll read all about it after. I'm right, you see, you don't believe anything.

REG.   It wouldn't surprise me. You can't walk down a normal street now or eat dinner in a normal restaurant. There's no such thing as a normal street.

JACK.   Another very interesting thing. I saw a flight of geese going south. You don't often.

REG.   Have you had any news of Christie?

JACK.   You can take off your coat.

REG.   No thank you.

JACK.   Take off your coat.

REG.   I don't want to.

JACK.   If you're waiting for Christie —

REG.   I want my coat on.

JACK.   You must be getting flu.

REG.   I'm not staying. I'm going to the pub for a double whisky.

JACK.   What I was doing was. . . You listening, Syl? I

was willing Christie to come. I got you. It's a near miss. And maybe she's on her way.

REG.   It is something of a coincidence. Depending how often you think about Christie.

JACK.   I was not thinking about Christie. I was bringing her.

REG.   Depending how often you try to bring Christie.

JACK.   She'll come. You'll see. Even if she doesn't, it still worked.

REG.   You haven't had any news from her? When did she last phone you?

JACK.   I sometimes get the definite idea something's wrong with her.

REG.   Did she phone last night? Or was it this morning?

JACK.   We're not on the phone.

REG.   I'm afraid I've no time for these religious performances. Nor has Christie.

JACK.   It's not religious.

REG.   That area. Mumbo jumbo.

JACK.   It's fact. It's what happens. It's how it is.

REG.   If Christie comes I'd be most grateful if you tell her I was here. To collect her. Do explain properly will you? There's no need to listen too much to what she says. Don't let her be an imposition. She might try to stay. It's absolutely unnecessary.

JACK *locks the door and puts the key in his pocket.*
ALBERT *by now has taken some Araldite from the table drawer and is absorbed in mixing the two glues. He mends the broken bowl, joining the pieces precisely.*
SYL *by now is ironing.*

SYL.   Have you tried to get her here before, Jack?

JACK.   Not very often, no.

REG.   Locking the door? What?

JACK.   Has she left you?

REG.   Are you threatening me?

JACK.   Has she left you?

REG.   She hasn't left me. She left the house. Purely
         in the sense went out.

JACK.   When?

REG.   Last night.

JACK.   What time?

REG.   Does it matter?

JACK.   I wouldn't ask, would I?

REG.   During the night.

JACK.   What time?

REG.   I didn't look at the clock. After midnight.

JACK.   Two fifteen?

REG.   I didn't look at the clock.

JACK.   Maybe she'll know when she comes.

REG.   You've some reason for thinking she will
         come.

JACK.   Have a look at the clock another time, will
         you?

REG.   She may have friends. She has, I know for a
         fact. Or money. She might be at a hotel
         enjoying herself.

JACK.   What did you do to her?

REG.   I don't think I got that.

JACK.   To make her leave.

REG.   Don't you allege I made her leave. You should
         know your sister.

JACK.   She must have left for a reason.

REG.   She doesn't have reasons.

JACK.   Is she in love?

REG.   Nothing like that.

JACK.   How would you know?

REG.   Why she left is between me and Christie. I don't like the word left.

JACK.   If she has left you, that's a big step.

REG.   Yes.

JACK.   Forward.

REG.   In-laws never get on. That's no excuse for trying to cause a tragedy.

JACK.   Give her half an hour. I should take off your coat.

REG.   Would you mind opening the door, please? I said, Jack would you kindly open the door?

ALBERT.   What do you mean I'm impossible to live with?

SYL.   I'm thirty next week. I think 'Where am I getting?' I'm not that good a dancer. If I haven't had a child in the next five years, I'm not likely to have one at all. That's okay.

ALBERT.   Five years is a long time.

SYL.   Yes, it's okay. So long as I'm clear about it.

ALBERT.   I'd say you were a very good dancer.

SYL.   Not to give up everything else. Not great.

ALBERT.   You get work.

SYL.   That's all I was saying.

ALBERT.   So who do we know that's great?

SYL.   It is up to you as well you know.

ALBERT.   Great, what a concept. Do you want a mob, or is it posterity?

SYL.   I'm talking about if my work's nothing and a child would be something.

JACK. Everyone's work is nothing. What do you think? It's profit for the dinosaurs.

SYL. Well then.

ALBERT. Your child too. Tinned dinner for tyrannosaurus rex. There is nothing except make them extinct. I wouldn't want it to spend half its life in prison.

SYL. You're getting paranoid, Albert.

ALBERT. Yes, I know. It doesn't mean they're not after me.

SYL. I wouldn't want its father to be a lunatic.

ALBERT. I'm not doing my flu any good getting cold feet.

SYL. If I make up my mind to come off the pill, I've made up my mind.

ALBERT. Why is it every time I look out of the window there's a policeman riding past on a horse?

SYL. I could switch to the safe period and let it be an accident.

ALBERT. I'm happy to be a father any time. I wouldn't make a very good mother.

SYL. Go and get some dry socks on.

ALBERT goes out, taking the pile of ironed clothes. The door's not locked. SYL puts the ironing board away.

REG. Sorry I can't offer you a chocolate. It's a present for Christie.

REG tries the door. It's locked. JACK goes to SYL and they kiss.

Let me out of here. Is it some kind of joke? Christie and I are expected to dinner with our likely future managing director. He has a charming American wife who's going to be most put out. You have to meet expectations. I can't afford to be thought unreliable. I've already been passed over because Christie gave

me an air of being . . . of not being . . . some
wives are an asset. She has the looks when she
wants to but she never. . . . If Christie's not
here I must get to a telephone. I could phone
from the pub. It's bad enough that I'm going
to have to fib. Christie makes it very hard to
be straightforward. I was brought up black
and white and now I'm always. . . . But if I
leave it till the last minute I'll have to think of
a really outrageous lie. I'll have to invent a
whole car accident with which roads and what
kind of vehicle.

JACK *(to* SYL*)*.   When shall we leave?

SYL.   Not before the end of next week.

JACK.   When are we going to tell him?

SYL.   Not yet.

JACK.   It was better when we lived in the country. I
could read your mind easy in those days.

REG.   Jack was an employee of mine. I fired him. He
used to steal.

JACK.   Paper clips.

REG.   Petty cash.

JACK.   Now and then.

REG.   I bought you a Christmas present last year. A
pot of candied ginger from Fortnum's. But
Christie and I ate it ourselves since we didn't
see you. She didn't ask to see you. She doesn't
refer to you by name.

SYL.   Jack never talks about Christie.

JACK.   If I'm dreaming and there's somebody with
me in the dream, it's usually her, that's all.
She's not the main subject. What's happening
happens to us both. There's nothing to be
said.

REG.   Christie never dreams about you.

ALBERT *comes back, wearing the same odd socks*
as JACK.
REG *gets to the door before* ALBERT *shuts it.*

I never said a word to the police. We are
relations and I've got standards. It's not my fault
we're not friends. Christie needs me. That's the
factor you don't bear in mind.

REG *goes.*
ALBERT *goes to the window.*

ALBERT.   Helicopter. What did I tell you? In the event of
a civil emergency they'd have us rounded up
and off into the sky before we knew what we'd
started. They can land troops in your back
garden. Do you realise if I left my job now no
one would employ me? I'm known of. Last
Tuesday a helicopter came down on a waste
lot not half a mile from here and arrested a
man.

JACK *starts shelling peas into the bowl* ALBERT
mended.
SYL *shuffles cards.*

SYL.   Pick a card.

JACK *picks a card.*

JACK.   You can't do that trick.

SYL.   Put it back.

JACK *puts it back.*
SYL *shuffles the pack.*

SYL.   Where in the pack would you like your card to
go?

JACK.   You're not going to get it right.

SYL.   Tell it where to move.

JACK.   Tenth from the top.

SYL.   We'll just make sure it's not tenth from the top
already.

SYL *deals ten cards, showing* JACK *the tenth.*

SYL.	Come on, look at it.
JACK.	Of course it's not.
SYL.	Right then. Tell it to move.

SYL puts the dealt cards back on top of the pack.

JACK.	Move, card.
SYL.	Right, I felt it go. Here we are then. One. Two. Three. Four. Five. Six. Seven. Eight. Nine. Ten. Four of hearts.
JACK.	Told you.
SYL.	Four of hearts.
JACK.	Seven of spades.
SYL.	Honest? Shit. Look, here it is, the next card.
JACK.	You're not magic.
SYL.	You still don't know how I did it.
JACK.	You didn't do it.
SYL.	I can't count, that's all. I did the trick.

SYL deals Patience and plays.
ALBERT joins in over her shoulder.

ALBERT.	You could get a job.
JACK.	I'm trying to get a job.
ALBERT.	Like hell.
SYL.	He is.
ALBERT.	What have you signed on as this time? An elephant trainer?
SYL.	He went after two jobs this morning and they'd both gone.
ALBERT.	I already know you're on his side.
SYL.	I start work myself on Monday.
JACK.	Albert secretly wants to be rich and famous. He's got a lingering weakness for the work ethic. His grandmother was a lady.

ALBERT.   I've given up a wife and children.

JACK.   Yes, but why?

ALBERT.   For you mainly.

JACK.   Before you met me.

ALBERT.   I could have gone back if I hadn't met you.

JACK.   She wasn't going to have you back once she'd got married.

SYL.   Would you rather be living with her?

ALBERT.   I've never said that.

SYL.   Then what do you keep going on about it for?

ALBERT.   It was twelve years —

SYL.   It's over.

ALBERT.   She's still alive. Our children are still alive.

SYL.   You see your children.

ALBERT.   I see my children.

SYL.   Don't blame Jack.

ALBERT.   He could at least believe I love him.

JACK.   I don't believe anyone's after you. I don't think you believe it.

ALBERT.   I've got nothing. I get frightened. What do I wake up into every morning?

JACK.   You don't look at me.

ALBERT.   I am looking at you.

             DEL *comes in*.

DEL.   Took me two days getting here so I'm not leaving yet.

SYL.   Del, come in.

DEL.   Come to tell you bastards what I think of you.

JACK.   I think we've already some idea of that. Why not have a cup of tea.

             DEL *knocks the cards on to the floor*.

ALBERT.   Sit down, Del.

DEL.   You sit down. *Sit down*. Thought you were rid of me. Did you think at all? Did you? Did you think of me? Wonder how old Del is. Hope old Del's making out. *Hell*. Slammed out, what a relief eh? All that trouble gone, stretching your legs, settling your bums deeper in your cushions, clearing your heads. Del's out there some place, he's gone, he's not here thank God, hope he's well. Oh yeah, I do hope he's feeling fine and making out and *fucking derelicts you are, no*. You owe me money too. I paid the milk bill before I left and nobody paid their share. I want thirty pence from each of you for the principle. Let Del do it. I *will not*. Two hours in the rain waiting for my last lift to get here and tell you. Which one of you would wait two hours in the rain for me? Which one of you would sit two hours in a warm room with me? Garbage disposal units. Necrophiliacs. Media substitutes. You have all lied to me. Sometimes together, sometimes separately. You don't correlate. I've made lists.

SYL.   Del —

DEL.   Who did you last fuck?

JACK.   Where have you come from?

SYL.   Fucked Jack, okay?

DEL.   Coming back down a Mobius strip motorway ever since I left. You thought I was on the other side but all the time I was . . . Mobius strip, right?

ALBERT.   Get your wet hat off, Del. You're staying the night, there's time for all of it.

DEL.   Paper, scissors, Sellotape.

SYL.   I know what a Mobius —

DEL.   *Scissors*.

JACK puts 30p on the table.
SYL gets paper, scissors and Sellotape from the
drawer.

From the middle of July I was squeezed out.
There was every kind of alliance. Albert and
and Jack. Jack and Syl. Syl and Albert, Albert
and Jack and Syl. But no Del. Where was Del?
When I think what expectations. Never again.
Utopia means nowhere, right?

SYL.   You weren't asked to go. You were asked to stay.

DEL.   Settlers fled to America from persecution. Away
from the tyrannies of governments and
religions. New World. Think of the longing that
got them on to those ships. Brotherhood, vision,
pursuit of happiness. And what do they do soon
as they get there? Slaughter Indians.

DEL starts making a Mobius strip.

SYL.   I already know what a Mobius strip is.

DEL.   And we were the settlers. And we were the
Indians. Bloody massacre. And I still get that
vision. I get on ships. But now I know at the
same time how it ends.

JACK.   Paid my debt, okay?

DEL.   Mobius strip.

DEL holds the strip up and runs his finger round
it.

You thought you'd get on the other side from
me. But I can fly over spaghetti junction and
speed up behind blowing my horn and crowd
you buggers into the ditch.

JACK.   Would you like to try making a specific
accusation?

DEL.   Everything I ever said to you, Jack, you repeated
to Albert. And you got it wrong. I don't mind
that, nothing's exclusive. I don't want
individuality. But you gave me an individuality
and the wrong sodding one. Who was this Del

character you talked about? I never met him. You lived with him, not me. You stole his clothes. That's my shirt you're wearing now. Don't let it bother you, I've got a shirt. Just so you know. My books are still here for you to read. I've given up reading. You haven't. You get the benefit. You live off me. I put in far more than anyone. And I want it back. Not just my jacket. Energy. It's my charge running this place and I'm switching off. You can all die of darkness and hypothermia. You think I like being like this? This is what I'm like. My ideal would be for me to feel loving kindness to you all and harmony with the sodding Way. Look at me. Shaking. Shouting. See why I hate you.

ALBERT. Think you didn't do any damage?

DEL. Nothing to what I'm going to do, mate.

SYL. Del, what have we done? We didn't.

DEL. You don't remember. I believe that. But I can't continually wake up every day as if the day before hadn't happened. Sometimes, yes, but not every day. You owe me thirty pence. Thank you, Jack, it makes a start. I've kept lists, you see. I've got a diary. Forgetting won't get you out of it. I can put a date and place to everything. I want an explanation.

ALBERT. We're glad to see you.

ALBERT touches DEL.

DEL. Sod off.

After a moment DEL goes to JACK and embraces him.

JACK. Get out of that wet coat, will you?

SYL embraces DEL and JACK.

DEL. Still want a fucking explanation don't I. And apologies.

DEL takes off his coat and ALBERT takes it. DEL kisses ALBERT.

SYL starts picking cards up off the floor.

SYL.   Sorry, Del.

DEL starts to cry and stops. He cuts round the middle of the Mobius strip so it makes a large one.

DEL.   Lived with a girl in Sheffield for two months. Beautiful girl.

SYL.   What went wrong?

DEL.   She got to know me, didn't she.

ALBERT.   Why is it every time I look out of the window there's a policeman walking past?

DEL.   You're paranoid, that's why. It brings them. Think of it like magnetism.

DEL takes the cards and shuffles them.

DEL.   Pick a card.

SYL.   I can do this trick.

SYL picks a card and puts it back.
DEL shuffles.

DEL.   Where in the pack would you like your card to go?

SYL.   Say tenth from the top. I know this trick.

DEL deals ten cards, showing SYL the tenth.

DEL.   So it's not there yet, right?

SYL.   Del —

DEL.   Right?

SYL.   Right.

DEL puts the dealt cards on top of the pack.

DEL.   Tell it to move. Will it to move. Move it.

SYL.   Yup.

DEL.   You got beautiful willpower. Move mountains with that. Here we go.

DEL counts out ten cards.

	Queen of spades, right?
SYL.	Queen of spades.
ALBERT.	How do you do that?
DEL.	Magic.
ALBERT.	I mean really.
JACK.	Magic. A three-year-old child could tell you that.

JACK goes out.

ALBERT.   Long correspondence with the council. I got quite literate. I speak fluent jargonese like a native of the town hall, but translated we can stay till the builders come in the autumn, right, which further translated means at least two years. I've got all the letters here if you want to see. Copies of my letters. I kept on top of it, it's chronological.

ALBERT gets a folder of letters out of the drawer and gives it to DEL.

DEL.   It was better living in the country. All went wrong once we got here.

ALBERT.   Away from it all yuk. Back to ugh nature. Saving our pow wham souls zap.

DEL.   City's so fucking ugly.

ALBERT.   So are you.

DEL.   Comes of living in cities.

ALBERT.   Somebody has to.

DEL.   Changing it are you? Imperceptibly? It didn't strike me the minute I arrived, Albert's pamphlets and meetings are making all the difference. I didn't spot anyone transfigured. But I dare say the membership's rising. Consciousness is raised. Is it?

ALBERT.   Yes, it is.

DEL.   Cities are fine if you don't look at anything. Just use your eyes for not tripping over.

JACK *has come back with a tray of mugs.*

SYL.　　　　You made too many.

JACK.　　　 One for Christie.

DEL.　　　　Is Christie here?

JACK.　　　 She will be.

ALBERT.　　Get away.

The dog barks downstairs.
CHRISTIE *calls from downstairs.*

CHRISTIE. Jack?

SYL.　　　　You'd heard her already. You'd seen her from
　　　　　　 the window.

JACK.　　　 No, I'm beginning to frighten myself.

CHRISTIE Jack?

JACK *opens the door.*

JACK.　　　 Here.

CHRISTIE *comes in.*

CHRISTIE. Sorry turning up.

JACK.　　　 We expected you.

CHRISTIE. Don't know why I came. Stupid.

JACK.　　　 Doesn't matter.

CHRISTIE. Sorry.

JACK.　　　 Albert. Syl. Del.

DEL.　　　　We've met.

CHRISTIE. Don't let me interrupt.

SYL.　　　　We've even got your cup of tea ready.

JACK.　　　 Two sugars already in.

CHRISTIE Took a long time getting here. Got on the wrong
　　　　　　 train and had to come back.

SYL.　　　　There was someone asking. . .

She stops because of JACK.
During the next speech ALBERT *goes out.*

CHRISTIE.   I would have phoned if you were on the phone.
I wanted to make arrangements. The time has
come for decisive. . . There wasn't a train till
morning and then I got the wrong one. I could
have gone to a doctor if I had one but I can't go
to our doctor any more because they play golf.
You can't get a strange doctor in the night. I'm
straightaway in the category of nuisance.
Hospitals never close, but you might never get
out. I'm afraid if I handed myself over. Who
knows what's wrong with me. What would go
wrong with me once I was treated. Bruises are
the least part. I don't want bandaids or
manipulation. I want to be saved. So I thought it
was time I paid you a visit.

JACK.   Does Reg hit you?

CHRISTIE.   Sometimes.

JACK.   Don't you hit him back?

CHRISTIE.   He's stronger than me. I don't feel like it.

SYL.   Why don't you leave him?

CHRISTIE.   Yes, I know, but I'm very comfortable.

JACK.   You've left him now.

ALBERT *comes back with an armful of creased
damp clothes identical with the ones* SYL *ironed
earlier. He sets up the ironing board and starts
ironing them.*

DEL.   Do you still go to evening classes in mending
fuses?

CHRISTIE.   When did I do that?

DEL.   Three years ago?

JACK.   When was that?

CHRISTIE.   When we lived in Doncaster.

ALBERT.   Del's lived with everyone.

DEL.   What does that mean?

ALBERT.   I don't know anyone you haven't lived with.

DEL.   You can't know many people.

ALBERT.   That's right.

DEL.   Do you want me to stay?

ALBERT.   It's pissing down out there.

DEL.   Stay on.

ALBERT.   See how it goes, shall we?

DEL.   Day by day. By day by day.

JACK.   Nobody stays except by unanimous agreement of the household.

DEL.   But I'm one of the family myself. I've just been away for a short trip.

JACK.   That's one way of looking at it.

SYL.   Albert's got a real family with children, so he's got an advantage.

CHRISTIE.   I'm Jack's family.

SYL.   I'm an only child. And an orphan. It's not rare.

              SYL *brings the cake to the table and cuts it. They all have some.*

ALBERT.   It would be nice to have a family. Aunts and grannies and great-aunts and grandpas and babies and second cousins once removed and black sheep and ones you can't remember that suddenly look just like your dad. For Christmas. Nobody's got that nowadays.

SYL.   Most people have got relations.

ALBERT.   Not relations they like. Not relations they belong with. Imagine a family of relations you liked to be with.

SYL.   You belong with them even if you don't like them.

ALBERT.   No you don't.

JACK.   We don't need any other family. What are you talking about? What's this?

DEL.   I've got an auntie somewhere. I haven't seen her since I was six.

JACK.   You've got us. Seems to me.

DEL.   Even if I'm not liked?

SYL.   You belong in a family whether you're liked or not.

ALBERT.   I'm still not sure that's right.

SYL.   Is Del staying?

ALBERT.   I myself don't dislike him so there's no problem.

JACK.   Is Christie staying?

CHRISTIE.   Are you asking me?

SYL.   You don't have to decide. He's putting pressure on. You can stay from day to day till you feel better. See how you feel.

CHRISTIE.   I just got here. I can't possibly.

ALBERT.   That's all right.

JACK.   I only asked.

DEL.   Give her time. You always did rush her.

JACK.   I've not been in touch for a year.

CHRISTIE.   Why was that?

JACK.   One bit of news you haven't had, not being in touch, is Syl and I got married.

CHRISTIE.   White wedding?

JACK.   We did the state bit in the morning and then we had a party on a hill up near where we were. It was sunny nearly all day and full moon.

DEL.   That was the wedding. That was the celebration.

CHRISTIE.   I wouldn't have wanted to miss a white wedding. Nor any wedding of yours really.

JACK.   We thought we'd get married, we suddenly thought. Since she's pregnant, we thought why not.

SYL.   I want a big family. Thirteen.

JACK.   Will you like to be an auntie, Christie?

CHRISTIE.   I ought to let Reg know where I am. He'll have the police.

ALBERT.   We don't want the police here. We don't want to draw attention. I want to get the place wired up with an alarm bell.

CHRISTIE.   Don't want Reg here.

ALBERT.   Lie low.

DEL.   She does that. She lives under plain cover.

ALBERT.   It's only fair to tell you this house is watched. You may notice yourself being followed.

CHRISTIE.   I always do.

DEL touches the plant.

DEL.   Hello there, how you keeping? All right? You're looking good. Jack remember to water you, does he? You feel fine. You're a great shade of green these days. It's lovely to see you. You've grown, you know that? You're getting enormous.

SYL.   Jack and Del talk to the plant to make it grow.

CHRISTIE.   Does it work?

SYL.   It grows.

JACK.   If you don't understand something, Syl, just leave it alone.

SYL.   Fucking animals is bestiality, but I don't know the word for lusting after vegetation. You should see Jack and his plant gazing into each other's eyes.

JACK.   It hasn't got your defences.

DEL.   It doesn't ask where I was yesterday. Or if I'll be here tomorrow. It doesn't ask if I love it more

than Jack does or more than I love Jack or
anything. Totally here, every time, all the time.

ALBERT.   It's not a great conversationalist, mind you.

JACK.   Reg is in the pub.

CHRISTIE.   What?

JACK.   He came here just before, looking for you. He's
waiting in the pub.

CHRISTIE.   He doesn't know I'm here?

JACK.   He knows you.

CHRISTIE.   Nothing ever works out.

ALBERT.   You don't have to see him.

SYL.   You don't have to go back with him.

CHRISTIE.   I'm frightened.

SYL.   Of Reg?

CHRISTIE.   No.

SYL.   What then?

CHRISTIE.   Don't know. Sorry.

JACK.   What are you frightened of?

CHRISTIE.   Being alone.

JACK.   Why's that frightening? What are you frightened
of?

CHRISTIE.   Not knowing what's going to happen.

JACK.   What are you frightened of?

CHRISTIE.   Time.

JACK.   What else?

CHRISTIE.   Space.

JACK.   What else?

CHRISTIE.   Me.

JACK.   What else? What are you frightened of?

CHRISTIE.   You.

JACK.   What are you frightened of?

CHRISTIE.   Creeping bloody crawlies and heights, right?

DEL.   Too true, she's frightened of earwigs and balconies.

SYL.   I'm frightened of blood.

ALBERT.   Your own?

SYL.   Of course not my own. Other people's.

ALBERT.   No, I'm frightened of my own blood.

JACK.   Do you know why you're here?

CHRISTIE.   You a Christian all of a sudden or what?

JACK.   Do you know why you came?

CHRISTIE.   I was fed up.

JACK.   Reg been hitting you?

CHRISTIE.   Bit.

JACK.   That's not why.

CHRISTIE.   Jack, you give me a headache. I came for a rest.

JACK.   I willed you to come.

CHRISTIE.   What do you mean?

JACK.   What time did you leave last night?

CHRISTIE.   I don't know.

JACK.   Try.

CHRISTIE.   After midnight.

JACK.   How long after?

CHRISTIE.   Two maybe.

JACK.   Two-fifteen.

CHRISTIE.   Could have been.

JACK.   It was. I'm telling you. I woke up just before two-fifteen and I knew there was something wrong with you.

SYL.   You'd just been dreaming about her.

JACK. It doesn't make any difference at all if I'd been dreaming about her or not. If I'd been dreaming about her, that helps. So I sat up in bed and concentrated on you. I felt you'd better come here so I started to bring you. After about quarter of an hour I felt things were better so I went to sleep. Then all day I thought you were coming. But it got a bit faint. I spent another hour on it this morning. Then half the afternoon, it was getting dark. It seemed like a waste of a day, but I couldn't get on with anything else. I could feel you were on your way, I just got into that, you were on your way. Sat there with my eyes shut and . . . sat there, you know, with my eyes shut.

SYL. And Reg came.

JACK. Reg is a side effect.

CHRISTIE. You did not bring me.

JACK. Yes I did.

CHRISTIE. It was my own decision.

JACK. It would feel like that to you, yeah.

CHRISTIE. It was me decided to come. And you picked up on that and knew I was coming.

JACK. No.

CHRISTIE. You can read my mind, all right, I'll give you that. You cannot make my mind up.

JACK. Yes I can.

CHRISTIE. No.

JACK. Well, I did, so.

CHRISTIE. You did not.

DEL. Sounds like simple synchronicity. Nothing to get angry about.

SYL. It's just coincidence.

ALBERT. You've got to know what's a coincidence and what isn't. People don't look at you in a funny way unless they've got something on their mind.

DEL.　　　　If I go to the pub for some fags, how will I know this Reg?

SYL.　　　　Holding a very large box of chocolates.

DEL.　　　　And I'll say to him?

CHRISTIE.　Tell him I'm here if you like. He'll only find out.

DEL.　　　　All right?

No one answers. DEL puts on his coat and goes.

SYL.　　　　You'll find it's not bad living alone. I find it okay. I come and go all around the place. It's nice I can come here. But mostly I'm on my own and I can do that. Saves a lot of worry about being left. And no one minds if I'm not here.

JACK.　　　Come and see the plant.

CHRISTIE.　Jack, I came here for a rest.

JACK.　　　I'm giving you a rest. I want you to get quiet. Don't think anything and don't worry about trying not to think anything. Just keep coming back to the plant. You're not trying to do anything, you're doing it. If anything starts happening in your head, don't bother, don't wander, don't shy off, don't grab it, just see the plant. You can shut your eyes.

ALBERT.　　It kills time like a crossword, but you don't have to be so clever. And meanwhile the Special Branch are recruiting men who pretend to be killers to lure other men into killing so the Special Branch have somebody to catch. And then who murders that spy? Mercenaries are recruited here. If there's no policeman riding past the window, it's because they're getting cagey. They know I know. Somewhere I'm on a list. I posted two letters this morning. One to you and one to me. If your letter gets here before mine, it's proof positive my post's being tampered with. The next thing is install the alarm system. Remind me to buy some wire. And all he does is garden in a flower pot. If he thinks his mind beats fertilisers, why doesn't he

get down to the Sahel and bloom a few tons of
wheat out of the desert?

SYL.   He's practising, isn't he.

ALBERT.   I'm warning you, Syl. I'm patient to a fault. It's
            your life. I've no right. I'm not saying this
            righteously. Possession doesn't come in. There's
            nothing chauvinistic. You could be a man, I'd say
            the same. But I can only go so far. I don't take a
            literal view of marriage. I don't expect forsaking
            all others . But you and Jack are in danger of
            making me feel irrelevant. If I was to go, you
            might not mind. It's not a threat. It's not what
            I want. It's the direction. So think about it.
            Think of the babe. I mean not only, not stay
            together for that, but that as well. I hate to
            ask. I'd like to do without security. But there's
            none at work. There's none when I look round
            the street. I'm trying to build a new world and I
            can't get the bricks. Or I get the bricks and I
            don't get the labour. Or I get the labour and
            they throw the bricks at me. So if you could be
            clearer.

SYL.   What are you asking? Something impossible.

ALBERT.   I don't want perfection. Just changes.

            The dog barks downstairs.

CHRISTIE. Jack —

JACK.   Shh.

CHRISTIE. Jack —

JACK.   No.

CHRISTIE. Jack, before he comes. What shall I say?

            REG *comes in.*

REG.   A young man came up to me in the pub and . . .
            yes. It's satisfying to know one stands where one
            thought one stood.

JACK.   I got her all this way just in my head.

REG.   She had arranged with you to come here.

JACK.　　　This is the beginning of my life's work. Like Fleming's bit of mouldy bread. I'm a scientist. Was it Fleming?

REG.　　　All right, Christie?

CHRISTIE.　Yes.

REG.　　　I got no sleep last night at all.

CHRISTIE.　Sorry.

REG.　　　I'm only telling you so you can see how concerned I was.

CHRISTIE.　Yes. I'm sorry.

REG.　　　Don't keep apologising.

CHRISTIE.　No. I'm sorry. I can't help it. I'm sorry. I can't help it.

REG.　　　Well, we must apologise for intruding on your hospitality and make our way back. I had to cancel dinner.

CHRISTIE.　Yes. I'm sorry.

REG.　　　I'd better take you home and put you to bed.

CHRISTIE.　I'm not going home.

REG.　　　What do you mean.

CHRISTIE.　I'm sorry.

REG.　　　You want to have a little talk with Jack now you're here. You must have a lot to say to each other. Don't let me stop you, of course.

Silence.

Do carry on.

Silence.

I'm forgetting to give you these.

REG *gives* CHRISTIE *the chocolates.*

CHRISTIE.　Thank you very much. How delicious. What a big box. Shall I open them now?

REG.　　　Yes, pass them round among your friends.

SYL.   I want to work it out on the little chart.

ALBERT.   Hard one for me.

JACK.   Won't you take off your coat?

REG.   Thank you, no, I won't be staying long.

CHRISTIE. I'm not going home, Reg.

REG.   You're inviting yourself to stay here the night?

CHRISTIE. Yes.

REG.   What am I supposed to do? Stay in a hotel at vast expense? Go home and come back for you tomorrow?

CHRISTIE. No.

REG.   What then?

CHRISTIE. I'm sorry.

REG.   What are you playing at, Christie?

CHRISTIE. I'm sorry.

JACK.   What are you frightened of?

REG.   Leave her alone, Jack.

SYL *(to* REG). Let her speak for herself.

REG *(to* SYL). Will you kindly mind your own business, young woman.

ALBERT *(to* REG). Don't talk to Syl like that.

CHRISTIE *(to* ALBERT). *Shut up and keep out of it.*

> *SYL sits down at the table and deals Patience.*
> *ALBERT joins in over her shoulder.*

REG.   Come along, Christie.

CHRISTIE. No.

REG.   I'm leaving now. I'll wait five minutes in the car. It's parked just round the corner.

CHRISTIE. Please stay.

REG.   I've wasted enough time. I've work to do.

CHRISTIE. Stay just a little.

REG. You come now or you don't come at all.

JACK. She's not coming at all. She's staying here.

SYL. Stop telling her, Jack.

JACK. Jealous now?

SYL. I'd like her to stay, but stop telling her.

CHRISTIE. It's my own fault. I'm sorry. I can't do more than not go.

SYL. Stay here then.

CHRISTIE. Yes, I am.

JACK. Who's telling her?

REG. Christie, I'm leaving now.

CHRISTIE. I'm sorry.

REG. You'll regret this.

CHRISTIE. Yes, I do. I'm sorry. Goodbye.

REG. This is final.

CHRISTIE. All right.

REG. I'm not coming to get you tomorrow.

CHRISTIE. I know that.

REG. If you come home I won't let you in. I'm changing the lock.

DEL comes in exactly as before.

DEL. Taken me two days getting here, so I'm not leaving yet.

SYL. What are you doing here?

DEL. Come to tell you bastards what I think of you.

JACK. We've some idea of that. I shouldn't bother.

DEL knocks the cards on to the floor.

ALBERT. Sit down, Del, and shut up.

DEL. You sit down. *Sit down.* Thought you were rid of me. Did you think at all? Hope old Del's making out. *Hell.*

SYL.   Del, we've got people —

DEL.   You've got Christie. I know Christie. Christie
              knows me. You won't shut me up for Christie.
              She wouldn't have treated me like you did. And
              who's this? Your husband, Christie? You won't
              shut me up for Christie's husband. You owe me
              money, I paid the milk bill.

JACK.   You borrowed fifteen pounds off me, Del.

DEL.   Want it back? With interest? What's the rate of
              interest?

JACK.   Just don't talk to me about the milk bill.

DEL.   You think you can make me do what you like. I
              will not. Necrophiliacs. But I'm not dead, too
              bad, I'm alive. You've all lied to me. Media
              substitutes. You're not real people. You don't
              correlate.

SYL.   Del —

DEL.   Who did you last fuck?

SYL.   Someone better than you, okay?

ALBERT.   If you've come to shout, just go away. We had
              enough of that.

JACK.   There's other things going on here, Del. I'm
              talking to Christie.

              DEL *knocks the bowl of peas on to the floor,*
              breaking the bowl.

DEL.   Talk to me. Talk to me.

ALBERT.   Stop it.

              ALBERT *grabs* DEL *to contain him.*

REG.   I can't leave you here with this going on.

CHRISTIE.   Stay then.

REG.   Come along.

              DEL *gets free of* ALBERT *and picks up the*
              plant, tearing the leaves and smashing it on the
              floor.

DEL. Hate you, kill you.

> JACK *throws himself at* DEL *and they roll on the floor.*
> ALBERT *and* JACK *get* DEL *to his feet.*

ALBERT. We don't want you here, right?

DEL. You can't do this.

SYL. We're sick of you.

JACK. You don't live here any more. Get that straight. You've left us. Go away.

DEL. Why?

CHRISTIE. I don't think they like you.

DEL. Christie, I'll see you sometime.

> DEL *goes.*
> JACK *starts clearing up the plant, the bowl, the cards.*

REG. Who was that? Christie? How do you know him?

CHRISTIE. Long time ago.

REG. A friend of Jack's. Typical. Strikes me he should be in hospital under heavy sedation. I shouldn't think he's safe. In his own interest.

> ALBERT *is at the window.*

ALBERT. There he goes.

SYL. He just uses us.

CHRISTIE. What can we do about the plant, Jack?

REG. We won't be able to eat those peas, you know.

SYL. Christie, where's the baby?

CHRISTIE. In the garden.

ACT TWO

The room is almost exactly as it was, but bright sunlight is shining through the window.
The floor has been cleaned up; the plant is exactly as it was at the beginning of the play; the bowl of peas is unbroken, as it was when Jack finished shelling them; the cards are on the table. The ironing board is folded and the ironed clothes in a pile. REG's coat is across the back of a chair. The folder of letters is where DEL left it. The newspapers are as they were, so is the cake. The guitar and gun are in different places. There is a different picture on the wall. The jigsaw is as it was at the end of Act One. The clock still tells real time. DEL and CHRISTIE are huddled in the armchair, arms round each other, the box of chocolates on their laps, eating chocolates and talking almost in whispers.

DEL.   Haven't told anybody else.

CHRISTIE. Why tell me?

DEL.   You understand anything like that.

CHRISTIE. I don't.

DEL.   You're like me in that way.

CHRISTIE. I'm not.

DEL.   Always have been. Killer deep down.

CHRISTIE. No one ever suspected you at all?

DEL.   No.

CHRISTIE. So you think you got away with it?

DEL.   I did.

CHRISTIE. What if I told?

DEL.   You're the risk I take. Always have been.

CHRISTIE. I don't want to know what you do.

DEL.   But it doesn't surprise you.

CHRISTIE. No.

DEL.   See what I mean?

CHRISTIE. Was she a total stranger?

DEL.   She looked back at me over her shoulder.

CHRISTIE. Was she what you think of as attractive?

DEL.   It was wasted if she was. I just hated her so I
              couldn't see.

CHRISTIE. What for?

DEL.   What for?

CHRISTIE. Yeah.

DEL.   Have another strawberry cream.

CHRISTIE. Stop imagining I understand.

DEL.   I hated her because I was raping her. You don't
              think I enjoyed it?

CHRISTIE. Did you stop hating her after?

DEL.   I was pissed off with the whole thing, wasn't I.
              I blamed her.

CHRISTIE. Did you think she wanted you to? Did you kid
              yourself that?

DEL.   Something happens, you don't want to be stuck
              with it. She didn't have to get herself killed, did
              she, fighting and that. Look where it puts me. I
              couldn't consider being locked up and they
              mess about in your head. It was some time ago.
              More than enough you messing me about.

CHRISTIE. Do you think you'll do it again?

DEL.   I don't enjoy it.

CHRISTIE. Do you think you will?

DEL.   I get all this hate. I get locked on.

CHRISTIE. Does it seem likely?

DEL.   Doesn't it?

CHRISTIE. How you feeling now?

DEL. How you feeling?

CHRISTIE. Nothing much.

CHRISTIE stands up and takes her shirt up over her head so he can see her back, which is badly bruised.

Del.

DEL. Yeah. Who did that then?

CHRISTIE. Reg.

DEL. He find you with another guy or what?

CHRISTIE. No, nothing. He seems to need pain or he doesn't know he's alive.

DEL. Yeah. Well. It's wartime isn't it.

CHRISTIE puts her shirt down and moves away.

CHRISTIE. Shall we go away together?

DEL. Where to?

CHRISTIE. It won't last.

DEL. Yes, I'd like that.

CHRISTIE. But you'd want Jack to come.

DEL. Yes.

CHRISTIE. You could just go away with Jack.

DEL. What do you see in Reg?

CHRISTIE. He buys me things.

DEL. Really?

CHRISTIE. He really does buy me things.

DEL. Is that really why?

CHRISTIE. I don't like work. It's only like living on the dole.

DEL. I always paid stamps.

CHRISTIE. I pay stamps.

DEL. But don't you like him?

CHRISTIE. Tell me what you wouldn't do to get free food, housing, clothes, use of car, holidays on hot islands?

DEL.   No one's asked me.

CHRISTIE.   Surprisingly enough I do like him.

DEL.   Yeah?

CHRISTIE.   I'm tougher than you.

DEL.   You're what?

CHRISTIE.   I'll give you an arm wrestle then.

> DEL *and* CHRISTIE *sit at the table to arm wrestle.*
> *He gets her arm down easily.*

            My arm's shorter, that's all it is.

> JACK *comes in with some planks and a roll of wire*
> *netting.*
> DEL *soon starts doing the jigsaw.*

JACK.   Mr Fellows came by on a horse. He's lost a cow.
            What he means is did we leave the gate open.

CHRISTIE.   They jump out. He must have seen them in all
            his life here. I've seen them.

DEL.   He doesn't like us.

JACK.   You don't expect people to like us?

CHRISTIE.   The country's always hard to belong in.

JACK.   He thinks we're here just for the summer. I've
            told him.

CHRISTIE.   He doesn't think we'll survive once it snows.
            With the outside bog and one cold tap. He
            thinks we won't get the roof mended.

DEL.   He could be right.

CHRISTIE.   We're staying here the rest of our lives.

JACK.   I am, but no one else has to.

DEL.   There's nothing else much I want to do. It's all
            beyond me. I'd sooner leave it behind and grow
            some potatoes and not smoke so much.

CHRISTIE.   Give Mr Fellows ten years. Or his children might
            like us when we're grey and shaky.

JACK.   Leave what behind, Del?

DEL.   Whatever.

JACK.   Do you think living here is running away?

DEL.   No, no it's running to, I know that.

JACK.   We're not on holiday.

DEL.   I'm never on holiday.

JACK.   The best thing would be for you to leave.

DEL.   I do take it all very seriously.

JACK.   No, this is basic.

DEL.   I do understand.

JACK.   What?

DEL.   We will be new. The world will catch our perfection like an infection. Contagious joy will cause the entire population to levitate two feet off the ground perceptibly.

CHRISTIE.   Jack believes that.

JACK.   I believe everything.

DEL.   Ghosts?

JACK.   Don't you?

DEL.   I tried very hard one time to believe in Father Christmas.

JACK.   I believe all world religions and minor sects before I even start. All science and superscience. And that every vision can be made real. Before breakfast. That's all possible things. I spend the morning believing impossible things.

DEL.   Like?

JACK.   That you love me?

DEL.   And the afternoon?

JACK.   Being impossible things.

DEL.   Like?

JACK.   Here. Now.

CHRISTIE *is at the window. The light has faded and slightly reddened.*

CHRISTIE. There's Mr Fellows with his cow.

DEL. Shall we get a cow?

JACK. Can we milk a cow?

DEL. It can't be hard to learn. Children do it.

JACK. Children speak Chinese. Chinese children.

DEL. I want a cow.

CHRISTIE. It's going to be sunset. Anyone coming out?

DEL. I've seen the sun set.

JACK. Shall I come?

REG *comes in.*

REG. There you are, Christie. Come outside. It's going to be a most beautiful sunset.

CHRISTIE. I can see from here.

DEL. Gardening?

REG. I'm proud to say I've nearly finished the weeding. Two rows of lettuces are nearly ready you know. We'll have to eat salad twice a day all week.

JACK. Go on, Christie.

REG. Don't come outside on my account. I just didn't want you to miss it through failing to notice. It's a mackerel sky in the west tinted pink and a full moon rising on the dark side. The east. I only just begin to appreciate how the sun shines on the moon. I knew it all along. I did diagrams in exercise books as a child. The word 'penumbra' comes to mind. New to me then. Possibly in connection with the eclipse. One knows the theory but when one sees it . . . the sun there and the moon there, full, or the sun there and the moon there, half. I'm always delighted by the neatness. That it all works. And of course the colours.

REG *goes*.

DEL.   Do you find incest a worry? The fear of the thought of committing incest?

CHRISTIE.   We did all that a long time ago. We weren't all that good together.

JACK.   We were very young.

CHRISTIE.   It turned us off a bit.

JACK.   It's not the solution to me and Christie, Del. More something you get out of the way.

CHRISTIE.   We're related.

JACK.   It's not the problem, Del.

DEL.   All right, I believe you.

JACK.   Go and watch the moon rise, Christie.

CHRISTIE.   Come on then.

            JACK *doesn't go*.
            CHRISTIE *goes*.
            JACK *takes from his pocket a book about poultry and reads*.
            DEL *does the jigsaw*.

JACK.   If each chicken needs six square feet, right, a chicken house twelve feet by six would hold twelve chickens.
            Rhode Island Red is the most popular laying breed in this country today. Leghorns . . . they don't put on weight. Do we want to eat the chickens or just the eggs?
            North Holland Blue has table qualities. It lays tinted eggs and is very hardy.

DEL.   I don't think I could say I love anyone. Not like fee; any different than what I do.

JACK.   I'd just as soon you left.

DEL.   I'd just as soon stick around a bit.

JACK.   You're meant to be committed.

DEL.   I am.

JACK.   One day you'll just go.

DEL.   The day I just stop being committed.

JACK.   I want you to go.

DEL.   You can't get rid of me.

JACK.   I refuse —

DEL.   What can you do about it?

           DEL *takes from his pocket a book about poultry
           and reads.*
           JACK *takes a half-eaten packet of chocolate
           biscuits from the drawer and eats one while he does
           the jigsaw.*

           North Holland Blue has table qualities.
           Rhode Island Red . . . the most popular laying
           breed. Each chicken needs six square feet, right?

           SYL *comes in with a string bag of carrots and
           potatoes, and a saucepan. She puts them on the
           table.*

SYL.   Jack, I've decided to call the baby Albert. After
           Albert. Would you mind that?

JACK.   Only if it's a girl.

DEL.   I mind.

SYL.   All right then, Jack?

DEL.   I thought it was going to be a communal baby.

SYL.   Then we call it Albert. Because it's a communal
           baby.

JACK.   Del, I do think. . . I mean if Albert was alive
           he'd be with us here, so it is a good idea.

DEL.   I don't mind the idea, I mind the name.

SYL.   I like the name.

DEL.   It's your baby.

SYL.   It's certainly not yours.

DEL.   I'm not competing.

JACK.   I'm just quite certain it's a girl.

DEL.   There's something where you swing a
              thingummy on a string. It goes round in circles
              if it's a girl and in straight lines if it's a boy.
              Or the other way round.

SYL.   No, I like it whichever it is.

DEL.   Would you stop liking it if you knew?

SYL.   I don't want to know.

DEL.   Why not?

SYL.   It isn't either sex until it's born.

DEL.   It is in fact.

SYL.   I don't want to know. It's part of me.

DEL.   You're resisting progress. You'll be evolved out.

SYL.   Look, Del, just leave my baby alone.

              CHRISTIE *comes in.*

CHRISTIE.   I must have left my fags.

JACK.   If I want to call my daughter Albert, I'll call her
              Albert.

CHRISTIE.   Seen my fags? I left them somewhere.

DEL.   Want one?

CHRISTIE.   No, I'll find them.

JACK.   What did you come back for?

CHRISTIE.   I just said.

JACK.   I thought you were looking at the sunset.

CHRISTIE.   I am, I want to smoke and enjoy it.

DEL.   It won't wait.

              DEL *starts making a roll-up.*

JACK.   You came back because I brought you back.

CHRISTIE.   Came back to get my fags.

JACK.   I willed you.

CHRISTIE.   Don't start that.

JACK.   Look in your pocket.

CHRISTIE. I've already looked in my pocket.

> CHRISTIE *takes a cigarette packet out of her pocket.*

I didn't think they were there.

JACK. Too right you didn't.

CHRISTIE. It's an empty packet. I did leave my others here.

JACK. Where?

CHRISTIE. You've hidden them.

JACK. I'm not interested in tricking you.

CHRISTIE. But anyway I thought I'd left them here, so that's why I came back.

JACK. You thought that was why you came back. You wanted to come back because I was willing it and you found that reason for yourself.

DEL. Before it gets dark.

> DEL *gives* CHRISTIE *the roll-up.*

CHRISTIE. Leave me alone, Jack, will you?

JACK. Believe it? Do you? Do you believe it?

> CHRISTIE *starts to go.*

SYL. Christie?

CHRISTIE. What?

SYL. Do you believe it?

> CHRISTIE *goes.*
> DEL *takes a sharp knife from the drawer and starts preparing the vegetables.*

JACK. Do you believe it?

SYL. Is it only Christie?

JACK. The Russians took new-born rabbits down in a submarine and kept the mother on shore with electrodes in her brain, and every time they killed a baby the mother bunny's brain waves went *vroom.*

SYL. But you're not that close to me.

JACK. Maybe not.

SYL. Have you tried?

JACK. Not very hard.

SYL. And Albert?

JACK. What about Albert?

> DEL *meanwhile cuts his finger, not badly. He gets*
> *a plaster from a packet in the drawer and puts it on.*
> *He goes on with the vegetables.*
> *The sunlight has faded.*

SYL. Did you try to make him do things?

JACK. It's not so much what appeals to a Marxist, is it?
Quite wrongly, because Russia's one of the most
advanced countries in researching —

SYL. Did you?

JACK. And America to some extent. They think of it as
a weapon.

SYL. Did you?

JACK. The results weren't conclusive at all.

SYL. He is dead.

JACK. Are you saying I willed him to die?

SYL. Am I saying that?

JACK. What would I do that for?

SYL. I only said. . . I'm not. . . I don't mean. . .

JACK. What? What?

SYL. To get him out of the way.

JACK. Out of which way?

SYL. Me.

JACK. You've got a very *News of the World* view of how
Albert and I felt about you. If I ever felt like
killing anyone it certainly wasn't Albert. I'm just
staggered at your vanity.

SYL. No, but just . . . you might not have meant to
. . . more just to see. . .

JACK.   See if I could? No. What, see if I could harm him just a little bit? No.

SYL.   No.

JACK.   No.

SYL.   It was better to say it.

JACK.   Sure.

SYL.   Than have it on my mind.

JACK.   Sure.

SYL.   What kind of thing did you make him do then?

JACK.   Like look out of the window. Nothing. Things he was doing anyway. I didn't try. I didn't want to touch minds with Albert.

SYL.   I wish I wasn't so angry with him. He'd no right to kill himself without telling us. He should have said something. It needn't have been to me.

DEL.   Albert was obviously a schizophrenic.

JACK.   Oh, for Christ's sake.

DEL.   I'm just telling you. If you don't want to know —

JACK.   Shut up will you?

SYL.   He deceived us the whole evening. He might have been planning it for weeks. It's hard to know how to remember him.

JACK.   He might have thought about it a lot without ever believing he'd do it. Then suddenly did it without thinking at all.

SYL.   I can't believe he didn't say something.

JACK.   To me?

SYL.   Did he?

JACK.   No. He said he wanted to have a look at the river.

SYL.   I thought you might be trying to protect me . . . if what he said. . .

JACK.   Nothing about you.

SYL.	But he said something?
JACK.	No.

DEL goes and sits by SYL with his arm round her.

SYL.	Unless some organisation murdered him. Is that so impossible? Or like the police or. . .
JACK.	What had he done then?

JACK goes and sits where DEL was and goes on with the vegetables.

DEL.	He was totally paranoid.
JACK.	But he might have done something as well.
SYL.	Do you really think. . . ?
JACK.	It's not likely, is it?
SYL.	Ought we to. . . ?
JACK.	What?
SYL.	Tell somebody?
JACK.	Who?
SYL.	The police?
JACK.	He used to get very depressed about his wife.
SYL.	He could have said.
JACK.	He used to get very depressed about his kids.
SYL.	I know that.
JACK.	Well then.
SYL.	I want to tell Albert what it's like without him.

JACK meanwhile cuts his finger, not badly. He gets a plaster from a packet in the drawer and puts it on. He goes on with the vegetables.
It is getting dark.

DEL.	When I was in Finland it was light all night. I felt quite sick by morning. It was midday before I got to sleep.
JACK.	Syl, I ought to tell you.
SYL.	What? What, go on.

JACK.   I want to go away for a bit.

SYL.   Where to?

JACK.   Haven't thought exactly where.

SYL.   How long for?

JACK.   Have to see.

SYL.   If you don't know when you're going or where
           you're going, I don't see why you have to go at
           all.

JACK.   At least I'm telling you. You won't just wake up
           and find me gone.

SYL.   I don't want to have a baby.

JACK.   I will be back.

SYL.   One day it's going to have to come out of me,
           alive or dead, either way, that's something
           there's no way out of.

JACK.   I want to have a baby.

DEL.   I'd like to go to Finland in the winter.

JACK.   If you like, Syl, when she's born . . . see how you
           feel, but . . . I'll take her away.

SYL.   What?

JACK.   She's my baby just as much. You needn't look
           after her. I'll keep her with me.

SYL.   You serious?

JACK.   Why not?

SYL.   A newborn baby?

JACK.   Tell me why not.

SYL.   No, you'd be good at it.

JACK.   I know I would, I'd be great.

DEL.   In the winter you'd see the sun going round the
           edge of the horizon.

SYL.   But what about me?

DEL.   Do you want to come with us, Syl?

SYL.   Would you like that?

DEL.   Yes of course, it's what I'm after. Can't you tell?

SYL.   No, I want Jack to stay here. Jack?

JACK.   There's no hurry.

> DEL *gets up.*
> He and JACK *are looking at each other.*
> SYL *starts to cry quietly.*
> *The light is now the same as at the beginning of the play.*
> CHRISTIE *comes in.*

CHRISTIE.   You're all sitting in the dark. Why haven't you got a light on?

JACK.   Yes, and it's bath night tonight.

CHRISTIE.   Syl?

DEL.   We'd better get some water on to boil.

CHRISTIE.   Supper before or after?

SYL.   Did you see the badgers?

DEL.   Get it all on at once.

CHRISTIE.   Just one. Reg saw two.

JACK.   Is there anything else except the vegetables?

DEL.   There's a bit of cheese left.

SYL.   No eggs.

JACK.   Better shop tomorrow.

DEL.   Plenty of bread.

> DEL *and* JACK *go out, taking the bowl of peas and the saucepan of chopped vegetables.*
> CHRISTIE *lights the oil lamp and brings it to the table.*
> SYL *deals Patience.*
> CHRISTIE *offers* SYL *a cigarette from the packet in her pocket.* SYL *refuses.*
> CHRISTIE *gets a half-eaten packet of chocolate biscuits for the drawer and offers one to* SYL. SYL *refuses.* CHRISTIE *leaves the packet on the table.*

CHRISTIE puts a pound on the table.
SYL goes on playing Patience while they talk.

CHRISTIE. I owe you a pound.

SYL. No.

CHRISTIE. Yes, I do.

SYL. You bought the drinks.

CHRISTIE. Drinks don't count.

SYL doesn't take the pound. It stays on the table.

Are you cold?

SYL. No.

CHRISTIE. You're shivering.

CHRISTIE takes off her jacket and puts it round SYL's shoulders. SYL goes on playing.

Won't you forgive me?

SYL. Where's Reg?

CHRISTIE. I came on ahead.

SYL. Is he happy enough?

CHRISTIE. Do you care?

SYL. If he's to stay.

CHRISTIE plays a card SYL hasn't noticed.

Don't.

CHRISTIE. Why?

SYL. It's my mistake.

CHRISTIE. Sorry.

SYL goes on playing.

It seems to be working out all right.

SYL goes on playing. Suddenly she mixes all the cards up.

SYL. No, it's stuck.

They stay silent.
CHRISTIE *is about to say something but doesn't.*
She eats a biscuit.

Sorry about yesterday.

CHRISTIE.   That's all right.

SYL.   No, I'm sorry. I should be better at. . . Anyway.

CHRISTIE.   It's difficult.

SYL.   But I am glad you came.

CHRISTIE.   Are you?

SYL.   Yes.

CHRISTIE.   So am I.

SYL.   There then.

Silence. CHRISTIE *tears off a very small bit of
leaf from the plant and rubs it between her fingers.*

CHRISTIE.   Syl, what shall I do?

SYL.   About what?

CHRISTIE.   Syl, what shall I do?

SYL gathers up the cards and deals Patience.

It's all very well to talk about the moon. Indoors
it's just another bit of scenery. But out there.
Oh, I can glance at it. But I can't meet it. Can't
rise to it. I'm too partial. I can't.

*SYL goes on playing. Suddenly she gets up. The
jacket falls off her shoulders.*

SYL.   Christie, what shall I do?

CHRISTIE.   About what?

SYL.   Why can't you help me?

CHRISTIE.   I can't.

SYL.   Help me.

CHRISTIE.   I can't.

SYL sits down.
CHRISTIE *picks up the jacket and puts it on.*
SYL eats a biscuit. She doesn't go on playing.

SYL.   I trained as a dancer. But I'm not good enough.

CHRISTIE. Does it matter?

SYL.   I expected to be amazing.

CHRISTIE. I'm clever. But I'm not interested. I was always more clever than Jack. But neither of us was very interested.

SYL.   I could emigrate.

CHRISTIE. That gets you nowhere.

SYL.   New life. Pursuit of happiness.

CHRISTIE. No.

SYL.   This is already a new life.

CHRISTIE. Never knowing what's going to happen.

SYL.   It's all right, isn't it?

CHRISTIE. I get frightened. Don't you?

SYL.   Yes.

CHRISTIE. But it's all right.

SYL.   I don't see why not. What shall we play?

CHRISTIE. Snap.

SYL.   Snap?

CHRISTIE. I don't play cards.

SYL.   Right.

          They play Snap.
          Both win fairly equally.
          REG comes in. He puts the lid on the box of
          chocolates and puts it aside neatly.
          They go on playing without looking at him.
          REG stands behind CHRISTIE and watches.
          CHRISTIE loses every time, till SYL wins all the
          cards.

REG.   Not very good at it, are you?

CHRISTIE. Out of practice.

REG.   She never practises anything. Piano the same. She played the piano when we were first married. Not very well, but she played. But she never practises. I tell her to. But she won't. Now she's forgotten all she ever knew.

CHRISTIE. I'm sorry.

REG. Perhaps you'll start again.

CHRISTIE. There's no piano.

REG. When we get home.

CHRISTIE. You could learn yourself if you're so keen on music.

REG. There's nothing I'd like better if I had the time. I've too many responsibilities.

SYL. Christie's got nothing better to do.

REG. She's very childish.

SYL. You have to tell her.

REG. She has an immature personality.

SYL. She's a flibbertigibbet.

REG. She tries.

SYL. She does try.

CHRISTIE. Don't describe me.

REG. She doesn't like people describing her.

CHRISTIE. *Stop it.*

REG. It makes her shout.

CHRISTIE *starts to cry quietly.*

SYL. If we go on about her, it makes her cry.

REG. Yes, the more we go on, the more she cries.

SYL. If we stop noticing her, she'll stop crying.

They wait in silence, while CHRISTIE *still cries.*

REG. We want to help, Christie.

They wait in silence, while CHRISTIE *still cries.*

SYL. Are you going home soon then?

REG.   Sunday afternoon. There's a three forty-nine which gets in nicely. Time to get in the right frame of mind for Monday morning. I don't like getting home too late. Yes, it's been a very pleasant little break.

CHRISTIE stops crying.
The other two exchange pleased nods.

If Christie likes, she could stay on a few days.

CHRISTIE.   No.

REG.   Do.

CHRISTIE.   Not worth it.

REG.   I want to make you happy.

CHRISTIE.   I want to be with you.

REG.   Just a few days.

CHRISTIE.   I can't stay by myself.

REG.   I could come back and get you next weekend.

CHRISTIE.   I couldn't sleep.

REG.   The fresh air does you good. You get peaky in town. It's not as if you've anything to do.

CHRISTIE.   I can't bear to be away from you.

REG starts to caress her.

REG.   Don't you trust me in town by myself?

CHRISTIE.   Now you mention it, no.

REG.   What do you think I might get up to?

CHRISTIE.   I miss the shops.

REG.   It's true we have some evening engagements.

CHRISTIE.   Unless you want me out of the way.

REG.   No, I was thinking of your happiness.

CHRISTIE.   I know I can be an embarrassment.

REG.   I could never go to a dinner party by myself. People would wonder.

CHRISTIE.   It's time we had a party.

REG.   Yes, we owe some hospitality.

CHRISTIE.   I want to wear a very expensive dress. My nipples must stand out under the fabric. Everyone who sees me must get an erection.

REG.   We'll have music.

CHRISTIE.   But it's quite safe, because I belong to you.

> REG *starts kissing her neck. Suddenly he stops, conscious of* SYL.

REG.   Would you be able to come to the party?

SYL.   Send me an invitation, will you?

> SYL *gets the suitcase and starts to pack the ironed clothes in it.*
> REG *and* CHRISTIE *kiss and caress, at first passionately, then with increasingly cool and hesitant movements.*

REG.   Bitch.

CHRISTIE.   What?

REG.   Don't pretend you don't know.

CHRISTIE.   What?

REG.   You don't want me.

CHRISTIE.   I do.

REG.   You don't.

CHRISTIE.   You don't want me.

REG.   You don't want me.

CHRISTIE.   I try.

REG.   You try!

CHRISTIE.   You don't try even.

REG.   Things will be better when we get home. Strange places are always very tense. We'll feel better alone. We'll have a party. We'll go to the Canaries in the summer. No, we'll go to the Canaries in the winter. We'll go to the Greek

islands in the summer. We'll go to the Canaries
in the winter. Or we could go skiing in the
winter. And go to the Canaries the following
summer.

CHRISTIE. If we can afford it.

REG.   What?

CHRISTIE. Inflation.

REG.   We still have two cars.

CHRISTIE. Two old cars.

REG.   If the flood water reaches our knees, it will be
over most people's heads.

CHRISTIE. I find you ugly.

> SYL *has finished packing. She leaves the case
> where it was before she took it. She is about to
> say something and doesn't. She goes out.*

REG.   You've heard about the little Dutch boy who put
his finger in the dyke?

CHRISTIE. What?

REG.   She didn't like it.

CHRISTIE. I wish we could go home.

REG.   No. Not now. Never.

CHRISTIE. I'm sorry.

REG.   We must part. It's the only way. I don't want to
hurt you.

CHRISTIE. Please —

> REG *hits* CHRISTIE *across the face.*

Please, Reg, I'm sorry. We'll go to the
Canaries —

> *He hits her again and she falls over.*

REG.   I don't want to hurt you. Be sensible.

CHRISTIE. I'll do anything —

> *He starts kicking her. She huddles into a ball. He*

goes and sits at the table. He cries.
CHRISTIE gets up slowly and sits in a chair.

REG.　　　Why don't you stop me?

CHRISTIE.　Sorry.

REG.　　　We'd better part.

CHRISTIE.　No.

REG.　　　I'd like to die.

CHRISTIE.　Sorry.

REG.　　　We'd better part.

ALBERT comes in, his hands dirty from gardening.
He takes off his boots, which are caked in mud.

ALBERT.　　Am I late? I haven't missed supper? I went on
　　　　　digging. I dug the whole patch. I went on
　　　　　digging in the dark. I haven't missed supper?

CHRISTIE.　No.

ALBERT.　　That's all right then. I deserve some supper. I
　　　　　could do with a bath too. I'm going to be stiff. It
　　　　　wasn't too dark because of the moon.

REG.　　　What are we planting in that bed?

ALBERT.　　Beans, I think, and peas.

CHRISTIE.　And next week we get the chickens. I'm an
　　　　　expert now on chickens.

ALBERT.　　We're getting on slowly.

CHRISTIE.　We're getting on fast.

JACK comes in with a big tin bath.
DEL and SYL come in with big saucepans of hot
water, which they pour into the bath.

DEL.　　　Mind, don't get splashed.

REG starts doing the jigsaw.

ALBERT.　　Look at that. Can I have first bath?

DEL goes out with the empty saucepans.

SYL.　　　No, you're too muddy. You'll have to wait.

JACK.   It's only for clean people this bath.

CHRISTIE.   I'll go first. I went swimming yesterday.

JACK.   Don't get in yet. It's scalding.

SYL.   It's not best going first, because it's shallow.

JACK.   Clean and shallow or deep and dirty.

ALBERT.   Jigsaw's getting on.

DEL comes back with a bucket of cold water and tips half of it into the bath.

SYL.   Somebody try that.

DEL.   I'm going first and then I'll get the supper.

DEL undresses.
ALBERT hugs SYL.

ALBERT.   Had a nice day?

SYL.   Lovely. Have you?

ALBERT.   Lovely.

DEL.   Where's the soap?

CHRISTIE gets the soap from the drawer and gives it to DEL.
DEL gets into the bath.

Ooh. Hot.

SYL tips more cold in.

Agh. Careful.

ALBERT furtively reaches into the drawer and gets a chocolate biscuit, which he eats quickly.

SYL.   Mr Fellows came round this morning and gave us some eggs.

JACK.   We need a rota for cooking.

ALBERT.   And all the jobs.

JACK.   When's Reg going to cook a meal?

REG.   I have cooked.

JACK.   Last Tuesday week?

REG.   Just ask me. I'll do whatever I'm asked.

JACK.   You should just do what needs to be done.

SYL.   It takes time spotting that.

JACK.   If you keep your eyes shut.

ALBERT.   We'll have a rota. Write it all out.

DEL.   Ah. Lovely. Somebody wash my back.

            SYL washes DEL's back.
            *JACK scoops water from the bucket with a mug
            and waters the plant. He talks to it quietly.*
            *REG keeps looking up from the jigsaw to see if
            CHRISTIE is watching DEL.*

            That time in Finland I fell asleep in a field. I'd
            no clothes on and the sun was blazing. When I
            woke up I didn't know where I was.

ALBERT.   Hurry up or the water gets cold.

DEL.   The saucepans are hot again by now.

            *ALBERT passes a towel to SYL, who gives it to
            DEL as he gets out of the bath.*

CHRISTIE.   Come on, Jack, help me get the water. Jack.

JACK.   You all right?

CHRISTIE.   No.

            JACK and CHRISTIE go out.
            DEL dresses and SYL undresses.
            REG is doing the jigsaw.

REG.   There's such a lot of blue sky, that's the
            problem.

ALBERT.   It's too fiddly for me. Here, what about this?
            And this, look.

REG.   You see, you're good at it.

ALBERT.   I like it when it works, but it won't last.

            They go on with the jigsaw.
            *JACK and CHRISTIE come back with the water and
            pour it into the bath.*
            SYL gets into the bath.

SYL.	I'm tired tonight. I've worked hard this week. I'm a bit out of practice is the thing. I danced all right today though I think. It felt all right. Has the baby slept well?
DEL.	He cried a bit this afternoon, but no, he's fine. I might make him up an extra couple of ounces tonight, he's getting through it all in no time.
ALBERT.	You want a new teat with a smaller hole. His stomach can't take it at that speed.
SYL.	Do you think so? I'll get one tomorrow.

DEL *goes out with the saucepans.*
JACK *undresses.* SYL *washes.* REG *glances at her, embarrassed.*

JACK.	Come on, out you get.
SYL.	No, it's warm.
JACK.	Out.

JACK *tries to lift* SYL *out. She laughs and splashes.*

ALBERT.	Mind out, you'll have it over.
JACK.	Tell your wife to get out of the bath then. I'm freezing.
SYL.	Give us a towel then. A dry one.

ALBERT *gets a towel and wraps her in it as she gets out.*
JACK *gets in.*
DEL *comes in with plates and forks, which he puts on the table. He openly takes the pound and puts it in his pocket.*

JACK.	Hey, it's cold. I want some more water. Is there any more water, Del?
DEL.	Not boiling yet, but it's hot.
JACK.	Let's have it then, quick.

CHRISTIE *and* ALBERT *go.*

DEL.	Food's ready any minute, okay?

DEL *goes.*

JACK.   It can't all happen at once. Apple trees take
             time.

             CHRISTIE *comes back with hot water.*

CHRISTIE.   Mind I don't burn you.

JACK.   How hot is it then?

             CHRISTIE *pours water into the bath.*

             I saw a flight of geese this morning going south,
             you don't often.

CHRISTIE.   It's my turn.

JACK.   I haven't washed.

CHRISTIE.   Wash then. Come on, I'll wash you.

             CHRISTIE *washes* JACK.
             REG *stands up and moves about awkwardly.*
             ALBERT *comes in with bread and more hot water.*

SYL.   I'll give Del a hand.

             SYL *goes out.*

ALBERT.   Settling down then?

REG.   More or less, I think.

ALBERT.   It takes getting used to.

REG.   Oh, I'll be all right.

CHRISTIE.   Come out now.

JACK.   I want to wash my hair.

CHRISTIE.   You can't wash your hair in that. There's no
             room.

JACK.   I can lean over.

CHRISTIE.   It takes too long. You'll make the water too dirty.

JACK.   I'll go swimming tomorrow in the river and take
             some soap.

CHRISTIE.   I'd like to go swimming.

ALBERT.   Yes, I'd like to have a look at the river.

             CHRISTIE *undresses. She no longer has any
             bruises on her back.*

> ALBERT *puts a towel round* JACK's *shoulders*
> *as he gets out.* JACK *stays in the towel and doesn't*
> *get dressed.*
> CHRISTIE *gets in the bath and* ALBERT *washes*
> *her.*
> REG *stands by.*

CHRISTIE.   I saw the badgers tonight. Did you notice the
            sunset at all? Full moon makes me a bit wary. I'd
            have to let go of so many things to make room.
            But I suddenly . . . I don't know what I did. I
            just stood there and the moon was up. I saw the
            first badger come out from behind the gorse. It
            wasn't dark yet in the west. I didn't fall short of
            anything. There were three badgers altogether.

> *Meanwhile* DEL *and* SYL *bring the food in.*
> CHRISTIE *gets out of the bath.* JACK *tosses her*
> *a towel.*

DEL.   Is everyone ready to eat?

JACK.   We'll start and they can come when they're
            ready.

ALBERT.   Hurry up, Reg.

REG.   Oh, go ahead. After you.

ALBERT.   I'm meant to be last because of the mud.

REG.   I'm in no hurry.

ALBERT.   I am, I want my dinner. I'll go now then.

REG.   I'm quite muddy too.

> JACK *and* SYL *dish up the food.*
> DEL *sits at the table to eat.*
> CHRISTIE *comes to the table in the towel.*
> ALBERT *washes quickly.*

ALBERT.   The reason I'm late is the meeting went on so
            long. We've never had such a big turnout.
            Things are moving, you know. It won't be the
            same place in six months. Is there a towel?

JACK.   None left?

ALBERT.   No towel?

JACK *gives him his.*

Bloody wet.

JACK *looks round for something else to wrap himself in and puts on Reg's coat.*
ALBERT *dresses quickly.*

JACK.   Hurry up, Reg, bath time.

REG.   I'll just have my dinner since it's ready.

ALBERT.   He doesn't fancy our dirty water.

SYL.   We can't top it up any more, it'll overflow.

REG.   I won't bother. I don't need a bath.

JACK.   No bath, no dinner.

ALBERT.   That looks good.

He helps himself to food.

REG.   Come on Jack, pass a plate.

JACK.   I said no bath, no dinner.

CHRISTIE.   He thinks he's fat.

SYL.   We won't look. We're too hungry.

JACK.   If you don't want any dinner, don't have a bath.

REG undresses slowly. He gets into the bath.

ALBERT.   Warm enough still?

JACK.   Here, I'll wash your back.

REG.   Don't bother.

JACK washes REG's back.

When I drove up in the rain looking for Christie I could hardly see the road in front of me. What with crying and the windscreen wipers not working properly. So I could hardly say I knew that road.

JACK goes back to the table.

JACK.   How hungry are you?

REG.   Can I have it in the bath? It's nice and warm.

DEL *takes a plate of food to* REG.
REG *eats*.

That's good.

*They go on with the meal. Some of them have
already finished. They are increasingly happy so
that gradually, each separately, they start to
smile.*
REG *starts to smile too.*
He laughs.

.